DUBLIN WANDERING

T0359446

By the same author:

Landmarks
Selected Poems of Ned Kelly
Dear Nostalgia
Boulevard
(Un)belonging
Blue
Preparations for Departure
Cult
Distance
Suburban Exile
Symptoms of Homesickness

DUBLIN WANDERING

NATHANAEL O'REILLY

RECENT
WORK
PRESS

Dublin Wandering
Recent Work Press
Canberra, Australia

Copyright © Nathanael O'Reilly, 2024

ISBN: 9780645973235 (paperback)

 A catalogue record for this
book is available from the
National Library of Australia

Cover image: 'Outside on the Southside of Dublin' by Robert French
Cover design: Recent Work Press
Set by Recent Work Press

recentworkpress.com

SS

For my Dublin ancestors & relatives

Contents

Penelope

deepdown torrent the sea the sea
Andalusian girls asleep in the shade
glancing eyes primroses violets create
yes red slippers yes I will Yes drown

wooly jacket lovely hour coming home
nightwalkers and pickpockets quays dark
evening wildlooking laundry ride me swelling
pleasure dew danger dream garments blue sea

guitar bathing plunging
into the sea
mourning for the cat
young stranger

squeezed squashed sleep in the coalcellar green dress
rainy day dribbling along in the wet coming home
staring sleeping hard peach perfume pouring jingling
poking rooting ploughing climbing hanging

cricket match walked home
a stone of potatoes
curtain clapped dance barebum
tongue touching plumpudding

dark knocking roughness carelessness flirting
whistling Venice moonlight romps
smell of the sea saltwater flannel trousers
hot as blazes cat she rubs up drunker

falling up the stairs stripped love chamber performance
moated grange at twilight excite eyes figure wheelbarrow

Irish homemade beauties sparrowfarts mists voyages
drowned windmill hill I loved looking running twisting

dancing pigeons screaming
I blew exploded bang wild
dreamt of her firtree cove
bird flying below us

tortured rousing tickling tender finish it off
white blouse caressed them robbing chickens
crushed flowers bloometh handwriting singing
silver dress sundancing domineering

the coffee bottom ash pit trouble mahogany swindle
wonderworker talking Bushmills whisky bursting booming
always waiting waves and boats drenched with sweat
dancing sashes warm bath rainwater the levanter heat

whistling train
tumbling tongue
lips shout fire
smoother skin

milk me sweeter thicker hurt teeth mark bite nipple
kick or bang lemonade greenhouse nymphs strumming
marsala fatten laugh sucking in Grafton street bank office
Inchicore September champagne oyster knife combing

measuring mincing food and rent burn violet breathing exercises
bottle of claret stout at dinner hanging tender fingers cracking nuts
featherbed mountain Glencree dinner outsider swearing blazes
skyblue silk fireflies dragging canal lock teeth Irish beauty

boycott politics
thumping piano
eloped jaunting
in a train holy show

charming girl whistling peaches port flushed tossed boiling embrace
breaking tearing freak persevering hungry rain skulking skirt raincoat
brazenfaced skeezing begging tasting the butter hearthrug fire bracelet
excite him waggling laughing wipes water washed up potato cake poems

fuming housewarming dressing perfuming punish thunderbolts whisky or stout
confession on canal bank wildly pretending imagine knitting woollen Dublin
pressed by the Tolka singing denying stealing potatoes ruining blottingpaper
wrangle in bed covered it up slinked out flirting hides razor imagine dying tragic

smelling my fur
politics and earthquakes
great leg laid up
breakfast in bed

Ithaca

going to a dark bed perpetual motion upcast reflection lampshade
omitted lands and islands converge satisfaction triumph futility
separation alienation simulation exposure executed extended received

nightshirt removed clothing deposited chair retreating impression recall
walking failure gathering atonement brawl leavetaking mourning visit
cardrive nocturnal solitude removal desired desire Narcissus sound echo

occupied bed thoroughfares exodus return sleeper awakened estranged
avenger returned reborn passing land to land boundary waifs and strays
wander selfcompelled Everyman or Noman discovery black cloud pillar

polestar sea following signs lakes of Killarney islands of Aran Giant's Causeway
windy wilds of Connemara cliffs of Moher departure nocturnal vagrant time
obliterated Dublin London Florence Milan Vienna Budapest evoke melancholia

suffering in Bloom ritual of passage graveplot possibility received relief sleep
soothes heals lavender cutting notepaper envelopes Dolphin's Barn
bring sealing wax bearing handwriting concerning narrative himself

meditate render connect weedbeds Irish waterways local railways head of water
Powerscourt orange plantations premature emigration family crest coat of arms
fires of smoking peat unmolested river fresh water secluded fieldwork

celestial constellations sunset scent of newmown hay weedladen wheelbarrow
sowing hayseed tweed cap lawnsprinkler lawnmower sundial hammocks
fishingrods lumbershed summerhouse cleargrained oak staircase ruby plush

upholstered hearth oak bookcase baywindow houselights olive green thatched
bungalow walking ache inserted scratched inflicted sting statue erect nudity
tranquility consult candour secret document necessity of order flyleaf antique

letterpress Gothic Hozier's maroon leather melancholy pierglass embalmed owl
Connemara marble aromatic incense volcano summit extracted downturning
pain strain emerald ashtray piano easychair slanted horizon wayfarer apparition

diffusion lonechill remind bellchime handtouch footstep dawn retreating feet
hear bed in the grave the peal of an hour take leave bolt zenith stargroup celestial
sign organ trajectories mirrors attracted sign arid seas omens of tranquil tempest

render incite waning waxing the lake of dreams the sea of rains frenzy weighed
wind transit lunar solar eclipses death birth dominating meteoric showers
Galileo the chariot of David vermilion crimson terrestrial species satellites planets

Orion lightyears Sirius milky way moon nightblue fruit humid heaventree
emerged creature cat door exodus keyless citizen decimating epidemics
mines and factories solitary notches public garden residence sleeping mother

daughter admired showed vision owl clock hearthdreaming cat earwashing cat
lake in Stephen's green neckarching Mullingar Westmeath photographic image
skippingrope blond ancestry shocks crawled crouched risen sleeping compartment

moving uttering waking weighed abandoned dressed in green unbroken
kitchen window winedark hair melody ogham writing merge chant revival
Book of Kells guttural sounds peoples contact rain followed polysyllables

interrogated dairy shop duets chess or backgammon domestic wives summer solstice
boater straw hat purchased composed overdose hurries wheels thinks stands dark
corner fire lit constructed suggested drawn burden induce abode of bliss

home burns out modern art stimulated kaleidoscopes suction sluice
canal lock spiral corkscrew refrain village pump Swords allude play divulged
pedestrians Phoenix Park hackney carriages roadster bicycles tramcars

scanning rainy Sunday coffeeroom lilacgarden drank steady flow
jacket fissure contemplated hospitality accepted viscous cream
printed prepare satisfied risked electrical discharge acoustic report

inspiration shining thrown away cabman's shelter corrugated jamjars cloves sugar
tea port black olives salt pepper shed human blood absence of light clattered milkcan
kettlelid radiated water vapour conveyed primeval forests declining everchanging

lemonflavoured soap halffilled kettle watercourses canals rivers icefloes glaciers
tidal estuaries fjords sounds archipelagos gulfs bays loughs hail sleet mist nourishing
vegetation distillation of dew springs cloudbursts maelstroms geysers watersheds

tributaries oceanflowing rivers highland tarns artic and antarctic spring tides
seaboard waves ocean vastness watercarrier waterlover admire water bloom
subterranean aqueduct black iron kettle blue saucepan housebells father's house

kindled fires apparitions composed pyre knelt hearthstone extinguished
kitchen staircase hallway doorway glass fanlight candle lapse lucifer match
ignited by friction latch rise uninjured lowered grasped climbed railings

knock enter keyless couple latchkey trousers housesteps reflected suburban lines reclined
gaslight druidism dissented inherited magnetism discover music literature Dublin Paris
chord arc bearing left west Mountjoy squarewalking pace normal united follow returning

Eumaeus

sirens walk towards the railway bridge both black two figures prone prying possessed purposed himself alone tripped up kick tenor solos for Dublin's musical world handed a cheque lyric platform

flutter in the dovecotes the clear sea voices of sirens opened looked sideways harpoon hairpin whale trained caged headbanger hipshaker flesh beware of the steamroller speaking beyond the roadway

swing Shakespeare's songs respected father voiced desire the sacred edifice yielded sacred music fields and pastures new walk night air skipped the coast sign drowned spark trail Sligo potheen

Carrick-on-Shannon blood chuckled blarney bones freeze marrow pillow toast mermaids entertain wound up jump spoil home crux retiring casualties barefaced striking twitted cured copper Bloom

reflected astounded rooked homeless walking find idea waste scene flutter hanging bones incensed him miles away sustained mudslinging penetrated Erin's domestic curves enjoyed sprang coupled

viewing satisfy storm drink spirit moving him dwell posed figure intimated turning glowing bosom casting the north side coming back country parts rural beloved tenants evicted

carried by a wave cropped siren verge electrifying her shared bedroom proclaim it his downfall staggering blow town talk till climax sprang up aroused in coffin shebeen land lie sound

discussion ship tattoo return bone bred knocked off haunting ruled movements fortnight boots
change clothes his name mistake marrowbones coffin shelter lovemaking damages outsider

colts and fillies starts reading foot and mouth absence tickled nettled change reflected emigration
swindle lovemaking turned press puzzling belonging sporting forced reverting acts fiddling

throne jockeys blame touch home foreign fumes change country shoved belongs bending
to Ireland burrowing home coffee work wind raise hounded accuse flag stirring bloody

bridge battle corner revolution boast silenced Erin plunging vendettas south refuse
channel neighbours consummation blows downfall marked for Ireland

stay in the land of your birth down there in Cavan on Irish soil grow butter and eggs
grind some chanty song wrecks returning in Galway Bay falling composing gurgling sailor

vacated weather breakers Norwegian weathered fog washed in blood staring rambling ships
flocking the seas from abroad any ancient mariner spin yarns sea air stir national poet

clashed electricity concentrate remember boom nautical fleeting chest love lane streetwalker
sighed glazed and haggard cursing blood sucks Skibbereen roaming run off to sea sailed seadog

wintertime rigging home seaside contrived floundering the antipodes pastures woolgathering
boats and ships salt junk the rover shook Gibraltar land troubles weapon blade knives roaming

globetrotter above sealevel in the wilds of Donegal the garden of Ireland
push consort work sleeping icebergs circumnavigated extricated shipped

brokenhearted husband in shirtsleeves coming back runaway wife expected fireside
rocked a rainy night blind moon homecoming scene demolished his body screwed

glared gestures rejoined too Irish name singled out boarded shelter retreat singing
language redbearded drinking coffee cabman's shelter vouch strays throw fathom drowning

belonged hanging terminus slip raconteur go back returned father to seek misfortune walking
Sandycove professing space preying dodging crossing broken biscuits Winetavern street dosshouse

sleep rocks Louth farmer funkyish shade of the railway bridge barren cobblestones pubhunting
tender mercy burgundy Pembroke Road court the gap drinking age dangers of nighttown women

think of Ibsen dandered waiting railway terminus whistle tracks lane stonesthrow wandering

Circe

ivory cane kissing reading wonderstruck changeling fairy boy tide ebbs the shore
rough sands reveal conceal shady wood communes loosens tightens distance
ashplant curls stretches dim white breast shadows murmurs listens undoes wood's
woven shade Fergus sighs stretches panther vampire bends shakes slow sleep sways
mirth raises mounts safe home burying rendezvous Bloom in gloom stars prone

lift home sober hearsedrivers way home old friend down to nighttown drowning grief
faith laughs scene wild oats mumbles shakes winking wagging whispers watch notebook
whitearsed bugger staggering lady friend lurches insulted assaulted shoves tugging spit
claw hair blow barks crowd nosing fringe strike follows to the wall falls stunned fists
outstretched shouting forgive him drags Kitty free Ireland peasants and townsmen

Alleluia elevates celebrates a naked chalice altarstone light shafts fall gospel epistle
rises rains furrows ride laughing lasses skirts above redhot bodies plunge spring wild
leap arise the midnight sun albatrosses cormorants swooping from eyries clash
shrieking foghorns drunkards deploy troops clouds roll fires spring up bleeding deeply
waves blare banshee woe keens Ireland's sweetheart deathflower potato blight

Saint Patrick bleeding searches whisky beer and wine plunges sings rattling cobblestones croppy boy's tongue razors slit emerald provokes come home leaf nibbling absinthe kick unicorns slain dust levitates country shakes witness fight roar robed ancient sucks wears archway comes forward expresses professor discuss struggle laughs sit propping staggers back disengages crowd elbowing plucks swimming turns dream safe home balcony

handkerchief sign sky waves jaw bash shirt armour cricket flannels ear biff hail Sisyphus civilians brawltogether wrangle quarelling fringe scaffolding beach corner stop helterskelterpelterwelter bookseller Davy Byrne street driver gallops hot potatoes biscuitboxes cabbagestumps pelted gallops zigzags pelted leaping biting panting breaking follows dogwhip stride Trinity trousers drenched drag torn

railings sideways hurries parting draws lechers lewd pay urges averts house dismount jingling fog cleared off tilted tumbler spilling water mountain air shouts disgrace charge boat races ragging Trinity student water glass enters damage warding broken chimney purple shade gasjet lifted ashplant snatches witness tore coat rushes hall pays lamp jammed pointing follows stampede screams flees ground flame leaps glass smashes masonry lifts chandelier

expiring save moaning wrings cold water rushes out strangled breath sticks bloody bones fire of hell smouldering repent window fanning firstborn suffering jumped Dalkey train saved sang green trickling mouth choking ashes breathing women go curling shakes kicked tears meets afflicted tower smoking gaping sing toothless eyesockets bluecircled bridal veil torn orange blossoms faded stark red couples wall whirls totters bump lumbering Blazes fuseblue

bawling plumstained stamp hitching ropepulling bang steer think glareblareflare
swift leaping spurn fandango hornblower skykicking frogsplits waltz twirl wheel table
floor ashplant snatches Kitty roundabout room groangrousegurgling shrieks seizes brusquely
pianola Florry played jumps mosaic interchanging droops swirling weaving masked daggered
bracelets flutter breeze landshadows bloom dispersed twilight rising touching suspend

arch arms curves shaping bowing advancing glovesilent skipping girlish blue slim
goldhaired waspwaisted violet lights fade change glow rose gold falling minuets
fondles breastbone buttons twirls dahlia lavender trousers green waistcoat claret lapels
skates spinning kick inserts leg between curtains fleshflower of vaccination
fireplace prelude seizes lights time twirls heeltapping bobbing lifts beats hands

fluttering wearing cape purring gold pink drops violet beating foot ashplant piano
runs fingers cracking runs claps dance! dance! street noise singing beneath windows
potatoes turnips onions barley carrot coins dancing mutton broth torrent rearing leopards
blue eyes flashing push home night jogs rocky road stumbling gripping green jacket
rain drizzle leaping ride bolts touts stockwhips salmongaffs follow live staghounds

sniffing leaves earth runs swift buried grandmother country fox answer break free
swoops wheeling air wings uttering cries free! red carpet spread avenue street harlots
extending Beelzebub across the world for a wife love a foreign lady abroad angels prostitutes
gestures machine pollutes diamonds belongs holy apostles dancing gloves sailing pommelling
leaps the fireplace claps hat runs wine drunk forget confessionbox gazes sings glides bowing

flaunting cygnets brood tawny sherry deathtalk flushed reindeer mirror plough throat rising laughing strawberries cream New York Paris peaches geraniums whispering lovewords murmur play apply Bella splashing water dry me tosses jumps winks leans shoulder mocks crouches swaying sprawl whispers releases slow curves giggle writes rises stretches travels beyond the sea peers detaches moon handwriting caress

thumbprint lie coffin slaps lightning shiver shake blue eyed beauty read Hamlet throws chants midnight match melancholy light strikes rambling fumbling falls deep sofa bumps her carries lifts Kitty clutches crowns earned limps clasping leans talks money count table calls from the hearth pocket banknote piano smash slip hauls potato teeth coats darts ramble chords playing piano turns escaping crucifix barbed wire pruning knife

strikes sings lovesongs clutches touch deciduously leaves straw hay wipes broken dance yelling desire waves sighing waters nymph overpowers striding crackling feathered bluestreaked thicket wings underwood treestems cooeeing woodland homage hand rules rocksalt heather pacing stonecold ear electric light far out in the bay waiting waters cliff fall downwards gorsepine thistledown burrs nannygoat Ben Howth

climbed downhill rolled grass curtains flaxenhaired spring bloom flowers forest waterfall Poulaphouca sweeping downward sward break stunned struggles rise ring warmgloved cheer penned shade boughs cascade waterfall reflects bends sea Gibraltar during dark nights praise hair cure cheap pink paper boughs streaked leaves nymph hair unbound disperses incense smoke screens flame pyre chant darkshawled broken sobs weeps skipping wine

thumb bites your secondbest bed lie in it romp rain statue crawls clenches
clover armchair writing table wonderwide breaks swirling seawind blue scarf
fairhaired greenvested gold dress drive me mad drizzle duck coughing kicking
tables stoops pokes simpers bends smooth walk emeraldgartered brands handle touch
rap gavel plunges arm bares smile swell droop carry turf gilded heels fondle spank

drink dance pisspots champagne ruby ring bangle bracelets insist swear vanishing
gloating courting couples nocturnal strumpet in d'Olier street telephone messages
enjoy sawdust smoothworn cult of beautiful gilds Siamese cat converted Newfoundland
swooning tickling surrender jeers shirts thrift knees whalebone corsets smoothshaven
perfumesprayed garments yoke uncorks nurse leaping pray buttocksmothered thrusts

curse buy pinion bare squat slaps lemon currant skewered slaughtered suck thumping
tender drags break bleats alpine hat bowed grunting snuffling sinks slide left strike
raises knots lace Bella magnificence satinlined kneelength lace up buttonhooking
bootlace sea rocks dewfall rain winter waistcoat dreamed slumber flirting mucksweat
eat heelclacking through the mist overcoat conjure drawing crack tosses catch bites

whirls nibbles fingers doorstep chocolate pocket carry my heart zigzag ogling nudging
shrinking doubleshuffles blesses scratches robe sings rocks gestures wave unscrews wild harp
slung glides gives a cow's lick to his hair yawns coalblack throat sloughing plucks lutestrings
murmurs smites burst mob Nurse Quigley bathing jerks hips foaming laughs whips
shoulders swallow apocalypse yelps howls run grasps woman's bites covers shows

maidens monks sex secrets buttoned up ashplant Maynooth flesh song purr
find Moira pencil lawnmowers lute artist voice sing minor chord drunk telegraph
I will arise and go play grave flower passage dulcimer dark velvet rushes sliding dropping
draws back burned cries arches hunched wingshoulders milks breasts dry forest Eve
the serpent sting redbank oysters bring claws running backwards wandered dazed

shadow bluebottle rubs honey on lured whisper sublime pomegranate snip melancholy
act rosemary Tara honey remedy Slapbang! wallow hanker bread tongue coated deep
keel naked permit tumble flapper alley cheek forefinger twitch wear hip observe skirt
lingerie backbone thigh injection mark Zoe brown macintosh struts smooths licks
stands twirling flows fluid blue twists sapphire bare flame wails whistling green light

the ocean stormbirds seawind voice of waves weeds shells encrusted druid mantle
cold seawind broods searchlight boudoir flashed lantern Yeats or Keats lifts leads locks
portwine tramp confirmed voice arms uplifted shouts rolledup shirtsleeves the needle
singing stamps vibrates congregation angels cold feet join book rush coughing yapping
perspiring taut bursts thumps drifting fog blares gramophone over coughs feetshuffling

springs sail juggling thighs whirls thrusts somersaults tumbles the gathering darkness
Liffey waters bears hook the royal canal tickling explodes summer God sun Shakespeare
Kitty Stephen gramophone blare a pair of trousers priests Circe's or David's boa uncoils
slides glances nestling strawberry droops goosefat flashes ashplant sprawl Zoe clap bends
swinging on the edge of the table beats peacock feathers squats jade and azure chandelier

purple shirt open turns crosses threshold trips swaying consent rustle scents
lurk music luring love me love me not fluid cradle rocks peel velvet smiles
cash nods born bleeding bottle blinds drawn music letter Connemara goats
dusty brogues emigrant's handkerchief shrunken mute Alleluia chorus Choir
voices plague pestilence potato pray for us daughters of Erin kneel black garments

gunpowder sets fire split hands heaven drowned corpse shepherd travellers
carry huntingcap joining hands seats evicted Irish tenants in the devil's glen
blushes shakes rattle bridge bushranger's kit writes on the wall tide turn back
eclipses turns foot heals eats oysters climbs covers walks railways arts languages
redcarpeted staircase children embrace hairshirt lockets bracelets vocal organs

faint straw scourges wine preserved teeth rake green jerkin midsummer
Dolphin's Barn throws boot boiling roast lynch bronzed cities of the plain
stinking steamrollers Guinness's brewery drinking drowning glory fishing cap tune
railway tramline overthrow tears naked goddesses shaking statues mixed bathing
reform dozen of stout house of keys parks embellish suburban gardens

emerald tear choked beggar gives coat refuses raw turnip blushing waitress whispers
dances consoles performs milk flowing bending down photograph cheeks kisses leaps
throng bursts forward touch butter scotch theatre passes cowbones soup graziers strikes
poppies fireraiser springs trapdoor collapses ladder fall barrels and boxes houses razed
railway sheds demolished buildings monuments workmen dawn golden city credit charge

deploying yield drive green socks Dublin keys common ancestors Erin cheering outburst moonblue robes descends sparkles genuflecting homage fireworks joybells ascends stone northwest weather sunburst furze wren perfumed rosepetals crimson flowing long milkwhite horse triumph hosiers and glovers archery cricket outfitters undertakers masseurs vintners waving cheering whistling rainspouts gutters windowsills

lampposts standing perched sightseers thronged prostituted labour capitalistic lusts manufactured monsters panacea machines recline on Boulevard Bloom in scarlet robe congratulate shake hands aurora borealis torchlight procession leaps phantom ship river music midnight chimes distant steeples corduroy overalls potato weed swaggerroot stray hair twists coil deftly Zoe Dublin girl gold sepulchre roses disclose ear accent

rosewater singsong murmuring cool still white nude womancity sapphire sky burns cedargroves lakes shores shadows mountains leaping feeding music played cuddling pocket potato talisman heirloom moist lips hard trouser pocket shrivelled working pays accosts trips nods throat sapphire slip slim black velvet silvery sequins rustle flutter warbling twittering cooing kisses daredevil salmon leap in the air

engulfed wriggles winces foghorns chants yawns defunct voice of Esau green eye flashes exhales bomb speak loud dark iron bells toll terror bloodcoloured coiled rope nailstudded bludgeon Mountjoy prison citizens of Dublin public nuisance bareback riding fog rolls rapidly brass quoits jingle elevates exposes marble barefoot she swishes her huntingcrop spurs dig savagely in public streets flog dare Quick! time

shivery cheek shuddering shrinking stimulate circulation spanking warm dance hot
love danger squirms flay scourge stamps jingling spurs horsewhipping ride bestride
urged Paris boulevards Phoenix park shone vermillion lauded treasures ragamuffins
honour edelweiss sleety day steps wrapped inflamed command peerless globes
Tipperary arrest wrote charmed suffering sickbed blood mouth cheekbones

sunken eyes slides turning wrong persecute doubt hand raises lips gagged badgered
Hades howled down belt sailor trousers barefoot weak chest submission covers
shipwreck heredity place scratch stowaway immigrant Oxford beargarden catcalls
burgundy spinach cough bucket loosen notebooks mumbles complain colleens
strolled green boreens model young ladies playing youthful scholars grappling bairns
Dublin city falling rain refrained affectionate evening homely parent domestic return

black sheep clothing surprised shopping oysters play cricket pilfering station
smart emerald garters far above flannel trousers owing leave carryings street angel
university murmurs lip upcurled kingdom books lavender trousers palefaced telephone
receiver strides connected departure ring dispatches park fought shoulder arms gallant
gentleman Eccles street wife daughter scapegoat inebriated drunk woman murmurs

behind hand flirt rugger fullback forearm square crimson halter sign drummed out
of The Castle striking with a lamb's tail glass of Burgundy Waterloo uniform gallants
engaged crumpled yellow flower broad green sash name and address Mademoiselle Ruby
breastsparklers eye glint redhor knotted thong belly saddle greyhound circus life frosty tram
Harold's cross scolded ramdriver dribbles scumpintle knuckle growls barstool sprays

slime cakes beaks Liffey gulls storm petrels murmur crunching mauls stalestunk
corner shambles tongue begging wriggling wolfdog sprawls Garryowen stinks
wagging his tail money waste wreaths weed floats sicksweet cigarettes windows
embrasures doorways lighted dollwomen frosted carriagepane drawing Molly
phallic design Kildare street toff shock damages save office cash night collision

Malahide engine train jump Westland row double distance cover quick drunks free
our native land Wexford boys staggers a bottle of stout shebeenkeeper haggles
battered trunk brazen gramophone rears from lanes doors corners spattered
with loiterers Bloom passes growling shuttered pub archway standing towards hellsgates
read knew Moses mimicking squeezes simpers fetching velveteen marked Foxrock

coming home Neverrell won Molly in Leopardstown tawny red brogues
shepherd's plaid oatmeal lapel woodbine follows wagging walk in a grave secret
crows spy forward lurching hanging lager bottle wait on curbstone kippered herrings
rattling lemon answer tongue between her lips kiss below stairs cloaked in the pall
muttering carpet slippers shuffles breaking moonlight blue ruby ring surrenders

mystery games staircase ottoman teapot recall dear dead days give you champagne
playing housewarming wrist seizes hiding dance embrace black masks buttonholes
slumming exotic rescue short cut home splendid heat haunts sin pleasure slides away
crookedly slobbering Gerty bedpost strap writing ogling wolfeyes shining weak squeak
laughter runs stumbles plunges recovers rainbedraggled Bridie Kelly humming saunters

19

brightens the sky freckled face polish lemon soap diffusing perfume fumbles grunting
droops blinking leapfrog mango fruit goldcurb wristbangles slender fetterchain ankles
toerings jewelled gulps of air cold feet waiting scarlet trousers datepalms mumbling eyes
downcast potato cries out O blessed candlestick in her hand hair plaited blouse buttoned
staircase bannisters open hand muddy sprint narrowshouldered bring home drunk vulture

talons bearded figure sweets of sin bookpocket midnight rag and bones slips past sidles
swerves ragman bars path beast style beauty bootlace mudflake brushes curbstone trickleaps
Bloom blunders whitegloved trolley hissing wire headlight red fog winking bells rattling
swim grazing shout urchins burning burning London blaze steel foundry aurora borealis
gasps bending blowing fish and taters arclamps sweated bright hurries lovelorn chocolate

pocket panting flushed bread bridge tramsiding crowd lurches river seaward south
beyond fumes cesspools river fog creep staggers away scuttle dark climbs gaslamp
skills holds breast span la belle dame sans merci loaf of bread and jug of wine
illustrates rhythm gif tongues music odours shattering light flourishes his ashplant
enginedriver walking the railway doorway snaggletusks flourishing jockey cap crowd

close bloodlight lampglow blond copper Cavan Cootehill and Belturbet lane girl
combs hair room lit wander warrens scrambles up railings crawls sliding after her
asquat on doorstep peaked cap askew heaves hobbles oil lamp rags bones shoulder
grinding growling dustbin counting swings release gurgles dribbling forges murk
scatter copper snow wafers rainbow fans danger signals skeleton tracks nighttown

Oxen of the Sun

Almighty God excess baggage! Elijah washed in the Blood of the Lamb
blaze on seek the night Bloom toff no fake full of words stunned Malahide
rugger scrum leg before wicket raindew moisture impregnated punctual
fragrant chap puking onions gorgeous! Speakeasy railway bloke seduced

on the road pepper shake Druiddrum press guzzlingden hayfever regret
beefsteaks vegetables wheat fleece drenched toil ashplants Panama hats
remember evening lawn grow suffer pipe ashes fought wags mist roses
fruit clay bloom eyes behold calf flesh delivered disappear poet's words

countless flowers workshop enable condition inhaling citizens wanderer
Socratic discussion atmosphere brogues tweed chair vacant hearth beer glass
dawn recollecting scarlet orange-fiery winejar whispered glanced at her lovely
trees adore underwood hedge reading reclined blithe friend couch romp teeth

pollen fruit stone cooked drooped bloom chestnuts yellow muslin sugarplums
tear gold casket waved scarf outstripped reminded promise meditate desire
work encircled the Pleiades looms magnified dead sea sunken waste land
phantoms moan sagegreen pasturefields twilight descends blend and fuse

silence scattering son of thy loins illusion sunnygolden daughter entwined night
raincaped shadows royal university drizzling shrivels duskfall scented handkerchief
walking nipping morning raised gushed Westland row station share songs tramping
Dublin full of Celtic literature conjured portwine stain strife of tongues chafing

ploughshare indignant rancher challenges to violate dupe trembled blade fell
praising table clapping eating of the tree revert to Bloom borne with the fruits
charged pity seven showers poured drenching cupful well water wallet crust
head balance flagon of cordial blond fellow fume loaves and fishes drove home

overtaken by rain Malahide omphalos standing famed cure the town
in the doorway sprang spread heaved to fast friends an arse corkfloat

water running off him blackthumbed chapbook discovered himself matters
meddle in Roscommon or the wilds of Connemara never shit on a shamrock

sweet smoky breath sent ale purling timber wools slaughter shed
a pint of tears naked pockets fecking maid's linen behind a hedge
moonlight between his teeth ocean sea poetry Kerry cows tongue
taverns coffeehouses brisk search swore pains letter table feet great

fall of rain flounder and pollock catches written odd heavy breath
deliver languor scholar covey of wags sitting snug crush a cup of wine
bound home rain poured green Mullingar stage earth dance water running
Merrion green Baggot street smoking shower west wind sundown

evening hills turf fields bargeman coming in by water
stout shield place turn she beguiled that land vanquished
the bottle plugged up the voice spike knocked ribs crack
doom draught hall cowed lag cried word blow mock jeer

shook breast cage thundered crack of noise Thor in the street roared
crystal palace applepie mountain cavity wattles dwindle die sunder wail
plague Hamlet his father flowing milk return remember Erin stranger
generations tower amorous country delights remember mingling

named toasting waxing merry involuntary poverty
besmirched virtue in the womb rest should reign
from the Quigley door a pregnancy joy comfort bread
drink filled all cups leave bramblebush of the winter

wild manner drunken founded moonflower unicorn beast
witty scholars after longest world wanderings house feasted
most drunken in scholar's hall quaffed drink cup spoke full
gently stood by the door cry drank pleasure draught

poor swells mountain angry spirits aid olive press
bubbles seasand white flames birchwood marches
learning castle door opened to the traveller sore wounded
to be healed wondered to look on her face into the house

for to go naked from his mother's womb
as he came everyman dust on his limbs
sent from the far coast wayfaring swift
kindled blushes bloom over land and seafloor

thatch breastbone Ireland's westward
water gate wide wandering far before
babe born bliss gravity sweating
chambers the medicine art of the Celts

Nausicaa

Cuckoo cuckoo cuckoo foreign gentleman on the rocks looking at Gerty MacDowell
butter and sodabread and tea dreams return plump years heave under black hair

smoke Belfast snooze now wooden pen he flung away that other world
meaning all these rocks dark mirror breathe bend there tide pool comes

write message for her bread cast waters old copybook page mailboat pyjamas
red slippers dreamt curse poisoned mother forlorn home God wince laugh

drunken ranters goddesses bath house keys private evening clouds seabirds screaming
yacht like a limpet Gibraltar umbrella wildfire loose laughing blue scarf laurel hedges

gleaming everwelcome tryst faded floated fell violet gulping salt water beam
belt hanging killed in storms fly over the ocean back ceiling shadow playing

wind and light broken bottles Archimedes amethyst flashing rub dry sticks
together brown turf staircase cat bluey white sun shimmering water pebbles

bird hopping mixed breed pray repetition mistake sanctity odour blind tree
swallow rusty gun dew delivering breadvan overcoat rip tear shortest way home

longest run into yourself escaping distant hills seem drained voyage repeats
crags and peaks oil-painting of her full kissed shoulder avenues chandeliers

lamps ballrooms girls grass cut paper stone dew falling phantom ship nightclouds
scowl smile spray red rays run country roads through nothing hurt better now

glowworms change think dark distant hills twinkling ships fly salt whistle
rain damp in the Ormond mother Howth walk back streets slinking

run up a bill almonds lemons grass permeates diffuses strawberries bathwater
cream wonder she takes off stockings vamp perfume skin fine veil dark

islands mysterious connection dark cellar dance heat pillow perfume floor
spurs and ridingboots head back Molly sun stars steel iron movement fly

magnetism pulling pulled trot knock rolling hands brushing washing
Dolphin's barn rocks curve Will she? burst darting Wow! her calf swell

stocking mirror handkerchief drying ironing Grafton street sharp needles
jump lovely seaside girls satisfaction look back dark lane clothes fireworks

down there drove home featherbed mountain trick flatters gardens kissed
hand French letter in pocketbook Meath street girl moonlight stage rouge costume

home music weighs postcard some poet chap took off her hat to show her hair
flower stags lions garden fiddlestrings foot salt teeth devilish appearance blue moon

tableau write barbed wire kissing fingers whispering secrets neck locked
never forget appointment new blouse dressing violet garters fashion lovely

take them all off curves inside her lingerie a dream alive in the country in the bath
the moon beauty hot little devil delicate tight boots slippy seaweed stones

wood slipped hiding twilight going leaning back against the rock head bowed
she bent forward a little glance soft sweet raptures dewy stars falling

gushed out a stream of rain everyone cried O! O! gold hair threads melted away burst
the Roman candle that cry wrung from her rocket sprang girl's love slender arms

come to him looking immodest skirtdancers revealment wondrous
full view high up above bent so far back she was trembling

she saw that he saw skin caresses fabric suffused divine her face
almost out of sight high leaned ever so far back soft fireworks

flying look look blue garters match shouted look she leaned back quick hot
touch of lips imagine sometimes panting breathing supple soft hot-blooded

passion shaped legs beautifully revealed graceful caught her knee her hands
his hands tremor working fingertips she leaned back far trusted pulses tingling

eyes fastened her intention adamant come on fireworks the strand running
over houses helterskelter blue green purple sheet lightning free wild untrammelled

appealing follow her dream stretched eyes blue waiting flame mourning sex
the Dodder land of song share dying gild sacrifice coming down Dalkey hill

laughs lure fear silent tears misted slipping beauty of poetry
Magherafelt violet ink write Dame Street tortoiseshell ribbons

trove her thoughts write her poetry album confession loved to read dreams
Gerty lighting her window lamp couples walked the avenue past church grounds

lighthouses cry dusk ivied belfry evening bells Erin gathering twilight altar
veil hands shoulders blessed seashore steeple passed flying smothered

stifled cough destroyed the sandman spades and buckets smoke pipe struck home
thunder rage black countenance postcard shrivel filth voice leap sparkled conquest

blue eyes stinging tears lips parted confounded cat blaze scathing politeness
along the strand gaze man's face contour set fire to flowers waterworks quiver

accents measured irritable little gnat tugging came along the strand
swung her foot fell knelt to sing looking up watching never took eyes off her

ear itching ringing caught tripped running rip up her skirt
she ran hat throw tossing called down the slope past him out towards the sea

ditchwater drowned stained glass windows Saint Dominic
a womanly woman flighty girls forget the memory his eyes burned

into her distant sea coloured summer showers fragrant incense wafted surging
and flaming her cheeks a danger signal the face met her gaze in the twilight pool

by the rock bit her lip rolling down to her delicate pink
crept seaweedy rocks daughter mother angel costume rain falling

walked down Titonville road toss flushing crimson tickled cheeks laughed snug
cosy twenty-two in November cry lovely before the mirror Gerty MacDowell

yearns gnawing sorrow time slipped up inside out blue for luck
Gerty's undies hopes and fears ironed them ride up and down

in the mirror waterjug in front turned the bicycle silent dignity told her Ireland
did not hold her equal natural dark brown lovely wave silkilyseductive lustrous

lashes eyes bluest Irish blue witchery languid daggers drawn lemon slight
and graceful figure pronounced beautiful a fair specimen of Irish

gazing far away into distance misty blue eyes lovable red lips extreme cherryripe
a laugh in her eyes frolicsome breath always loaf of bread with golden syrup

cuddled rocking playing dabbling fold the world in summer evening

The Cyclops

Clouds of angels ascend over Donohoe's the terrible moon clothed in the glory
they beheld the chariot volley of oaths furious driving the gold cup giant's
causeway coat of arms silk umbrella gold handle seismic waves down the river

Pigeonhouse flotilla of barges escorted amid cheers Slieve Bloom
Connemara hills Bray Head Mountains of Mourne bonfires along the coastline
Hill of Howth lighted summits Irish pipes come back to Erin

the four seas silver Celtic ornament Irish artists ancient Irish vellum illuminated porter
in your guts lowering the pint heel sporting a circle of foam waves comely nymphs
tossed his milkwhite dolphin mane cute arches and spires and cupolas cornices

and pediments vaults and groynes multiplying unicorns candles millstones watertight
boots anvils bells beehives lamps dragons keys shells lilies axes loaves arrows palms
swords harps Ballymun and Kilkenny Celestine Dingle boatbearers readers

the sound of our shores a true word spoken south city markets love his country
widows and orphans Bloom merry rogue flagon boar's head venison veal pigeon pasty
servest thou rustic goodbye Ireland I'm going to Gort a bloody dark horse throwaway

a few bob Irishman citizen trade follows an illuminated bible Mary and Patrick
Gerry loves the boy has the bicycle love loves to love love your neighbours
life everybody knows I belong too this instant this moment by the waters of sorrow

Fingal's Cave the bog of Allen the rock of Cashel Tullamore Croagh Patrick
the Twelve Pins Glendalough Killarney a Kerry calf presenting Ireland
I was born here living in the same place for years a nation twenty thousand died

in the coffinships the British drove out the peasants tried to starve home
the land full of crops our greater Irish beyond the sea driven out in black 47
their shielings laid low the tragedy in Connacht we will have our harbours

full again with a fleet of masts of the Cavan O'Reillys the O'Kennedys of Dublin
the Galway Lynches the earl of Desmond the winedark waterway with our own flag
to the fore the green silk broad emerald revelations chieftain elm of Kildare

giant ash of Galway trees of Ireland on fair hills of Eire the beds of the Barrow
and Shannon far-famed horses Tipperary silver Connemara marble twenty millions
of missing Irish should be here rulers of the waves dark strong foamy ale

any civilization they have they stole from us the Irish language high and mighty
chief of all Erin we let the strangers come in swindling the peasants the poor of Ireland
stranger in our house Bloom heard nothing shackled hand and foot virgin daughter

of the skies a passage to Canada in a secondhand coffin drink our pints in peace
let us Marion of the bountiful bosoms ravenhaired daughter my singing wife
the bright particular star a summer holiday tour a treat to watch Dublin's pet lamb

dusted the floor with him the traitor's son violent exercise the press and the bar
declare he'd talk about it for an hour building up a nation Irish sport Irish games
in Phoenix park the commissioner of police forbidding the league going off

by the mailboat with his book and pencil the darling of all countries
slan leat brought pints kick the shite out of him up the aisle wagging her tail
hugging and snugging drinking porter teacups in a shebeen blind to the world

trying to walk straight the bitterness comes lurching around selling bazaar tickets
a swim duck could make a hole in another pint a chara guts roaring red ancient
Celtic bards old Irish wolfdog bloodshot eye from the drouth grousing and growling

hauling and mauling talking to him in Irish blowing into bagpipes sky pilots sober
Ireland free lemonade and oranges and medals colleen bawns on a truss of hay
froth of his pint pour all manner of drink the Gaelic league emeralds

form a fourleaved shamrock a skull and crossbones brooch requesting her name fair sex making use of handkerchiefs rocked with delight Anna Liffey anon a hurling match on the banks mingled salt streams sheila my own invigorating milkjugs

disembowelling appliances mahogany table quartering knife in a pool of rainwater high double F our greatgreatgrandmothers scaffold boomerangs blunderbusses umbrellas catapults scimitars poor fatherless and motherless children

broadsheets of torrential rain poured down Sinn Fein a hundred muffled drums the funeral deathbell unceasingly tolled a queer story led him the rounds of Dublin with a swank cigar on his lardy face a new Ireland ruling passion strong capital

punishment in the dark land vengeful knights mistake a barbarous bloody barbarian skeezing round the door Garryowen growling again a kip in Hardwicke street bloody eye tear parsnips in Dublin under the influence on duty wind wail whirlwind ocean foot on the bracken mortal haunts the eastern angle Mars and Jupiter buttermilk waves his earthname begob letters and envelopes his pocket prowling up and down outside smithwork bronze succulent berries of the hop blue mouldy pint

want bitter experience in sable armour rude yet striking art the mountain gorse the Russians tyrannise cause foreign wars markets on the rise drop the sky targets of lamb rennets of cheese butter butts from pasturelands of Lush and Rush the streamy vales of Thomond and the Shannon sieves of gooseberries and raspberries punnets of mushrooms pearls of onions tallies of kale yellow brown russet potatoes chieftain descended from chieftains peerless princes of Munster and Connacht

voyage afar woo eucalyptus sycamore cedar planetree east and west exalted murmuring waters a watchtower rises in the land holy wonderful strange citizen tea and sugar weight of tongue a bloody sweep be damned at the corner of Arbour hill dodging along Stony Batter

The Sirens

nations of the earth tram coming my epitaph seabloom last words
my country did not see sweet home too near too dear

knowing wet night in the lane so lonely endearing form
towards the quay straw sailor hat muffled horn in Lombard street

west hair down Molly shift her have mercy in Gardiner street tap tap tap
beerpull summer rose song fiddle that ballad upon my soul in the hallway

deepseashadow so lonely satiny bosom fondling mournful voice
prayer chords consented beauty no son she listens his brothers fell at Wexford

sideways mirror there Latin again the churchyard chords harped grief
came slow he knelt holy father comedown chamber music acoustics

falling water twinkling fingers played again gallants deliver the goods
her ear a shell lovely seaside girls buttered toast skin tanned gorgeous

Bald Pat the waiter who waits references Shakespeare town traveller seven
Davy Byrne's moonlight nightcall tambourined voices blending improvising

vibrations chords tune queer songs on that theme second tankard twang
Dorset street jingle human voice glorious decanted Guinness drank his Power

cider chords closed Blazes well sung soaring a swift pure cry serene
cry of passion graceful look she sang wore black lace full bosom

throat warbling perfume Bloom flood of desire dark invading idle dreaming
Cork brogue softer glorious tone tenors women by the score a voice sang low

leaves rain murmur touching ears with words endearing a beautiful air lovely air
all is lost now keys confessed rose higher laid his pipe to rest obedient wind

upon the headland a lovely girl ship sail farewell Erin we are their harps
understanding moist lady's hand mashed potatoes Molly threw herself back

across the bed laughing kicking too much trouble she drank cool stout
patience warmseated steak and kidney rock of Gibraltar ocean shadow daughter

Irish buxom lassy Marion Tweedy haunted quays playing piano in the coffee palace
the saloon horn blazes bronze tiny chalice drank off drops essence of vulgarity

elastic garter smackwarm thigh bending suspending peak of skirt
nipped quavering chords kindling the air pleaded a high note

communing appetite her humming lips hummed oceansong
eastern seas slowsyrupy sloe stretching her bust unconqured

walking warily a voiceless song cream vellum paper swaying mermaid
soft pedalling keys the elite of Erin Dublin's most brilliant quaffed the nectarbowl

youthful bard gaze shopgirl Mourne mountains whisky grace tempting poor males
violet silk petticoats sweets of sin saints above! bronzegold deep laughter breathless

flushed panting sighing blessed virgins laughter shriek sweet tea bidding adieu
her skin unbloused sunburnt bronze gold black satin sauntered sadly gold hair

behind curving ear wet lips laughing exquisite contrast oceangreen shadow dark
middle earth fallen deepsounding cold seahorn so sad lonely moonlight alluring

warbling full throb come! Fluted horn a veil awave upon the waves
fluted chords crashing warm sweetheart thigh smack garter rebound

breaking morn soft word look! bright stars fade long throbbing
pure call longindying call satiny breasts gold hair blue bloom

The Wandering Rocks

A closing door swallowed sturdy trousers on Landsdowne
and Northumberland roads two small schoolboys visiting
the Irish capital at Haddington road corner sanded women
halted a pedestrian in a brown macintosh passed a blind stripling
an umbrella blue lips hoarding Royal Canal bridge greased fingers

touched his cap towards Lower Mount street deep in Leinster
street a factory lass drumthumped music indigo along Nassau street
professor of dancing shouted the tidings at Dilly Dedalus a charming
lifted skirt in front Gerty McDowell carrying luncheon passing Poddle
river at the doorstep stroking Arran the cavalcade proceeded to confession

poor pa Dignam is dead ma crying in the parlour in Grafton street
a red flower and a swell pair listening to the drunk and grinning time
blooming all over cap awry charming Marie Kendall on his left
after Wicklow lane Mrs Quigley strode on for Clare street
a slender tapping cane frowning turned back along Merrion square

stickumbrelladustcoat dangling sailed eastward ships and trawlers
amid an archipelago Buck Mulligan slit a steaming scone in Irish myth
drove his wits astray call him Wandering Aengus Primrose waistcoat
whispered translated the horses shimmering cool shadow of the doorway
Irish language of our damned forefathers without a second word

much kindness bronze by gold joyful fingers towards the shopfronts
strode past crossed the quay up and down prowling salt green death
seaweed hair lank coils under a quilt of old overcoats who has passed
here before me? turned and halted by the bookcart the burial earth
immortal wheat Irishtown cockles sailorman sips rum dances fallen

archangels in the dark wormy earth winedark stones vulture nails
damn good gin a cavalcade passed along Pembroke quay hulls

and anchorchains sailing westward the sweepings of every country
walk on along the gutter the man upstairs is dead in Dublin
give it up father shrugged shoulders the air of the bookshop

on O'Connell bridge dancing professor a cultured allroundman
a touch of the artist hell's delights! a fine pair along Wellington quay
by the river wall he bought a book in Liffey street halted at the Dolphin
passed the musichall the column rising a new gunpowder plot
sack of carob from Wexford bring the camera Adelaide road

holding up her skirt a baton of rolled music grazie maestro
an Inchicore tram unloaded carfuls of tourists passed Trinity
slowly Blazes Boylan looked into her blouse with favour
blond girl's slim fingers reckoned the city rode lightly
down the Liffey sailing eastward breaking big chunks of bread

a plump bare arm shone flung forth a coin home beauty
a silent jet of hayjuice arched into the Dollymount tram
a young woman came from a gap in the hedge the stubble
of Clongowes field walked reading the evening
a flock of clouds walked alone along the shore

an otter plunged in joyous townlands seas adjoining
past Mud Island idyllic turfbarge towhorse bargeman dig out bogs
to make fires a catastrophe in New York satchelled schoolboys crossed
Richmond street walked the North Circular curbstone at Belvedere soldiers
and sailors legs shot off by cannonballs held out a peaked cap for alms

Scylla and Charybdis

cease to strive wide earth smoke ascended followed sun
over bridge arch ancient mariner fear between seas

mulberrycoloured multitudinous daughters of Erin
walking on most beautiful inquisitional drunken jesuit

mournful mummer dour recluse selfnodding
in the readers' room the bards must drink

wandering Aengus mystery Hamlet eureka! Dane or Dubliner
plants his mulberrytree in the earth silent witness returns

after a life of absence to where he was born
buries certain fathoms in the earth banishment from home

Bohemia on the seacoast makes Ulysses quote Aristotle
a Celtic legend older than history where is your brother?

in the old Irish myths a celestial phenomenon
we ask our childhood revealed in sonnets

in a dark corner of canvas his father's decline his envy sundered
on the quayside conscious begetting she read his chapbooks

vanished long ago pogue mahone! Hamlet and Macbeth
whom do you suspect? left her secondbest bed

the punks of the bankside Walt Whitman called it art
Oisin with Patrick gargoyle face contribution to literature

spend a few shillings drunk on College Green lower Abbey street
tame essence of Wilde last night in Dublin writes like Synge

the librarian said his own self ribald face from the doorway
the sea's voice by Elsinor's rocks two rages comingle in a whirlpool

Tir na n-og west of the moon east of the sun
how the shadow lifts passages with Ophelia

the ghost of the unquiet father in painted chambers
knowing no vixen illuminating views loneliest daughter

Cordelia our national epic yet to be written
his ashplanthandle over his knee gathering a sheaf

of younger poets' verses lotus ladies tend them
tumbles in a cornfield blue windows hemlock of Sinn Fein

passionate pilgrim volitional errors mother's deathbed
fly in the face of tradition flow with your waves your waters

cygnets towards the rushes a day in mid June from Paris to Dublin
a ghost between the devil and the deep sea Mallarme on the hillside

an emerald twinkling stone peatsmoke lovesongs of Connacht
banished the eternal wisdom of Hamlet deepest poetry of Shelley

our Irish bards in the shadow of the glen beautiful green
fields a great poet taking arms against a sea of troubles

The Lestrygonians

walk quietly safe gate cream curves of stone cold statues
straw hat in sunlight library Kildare Street a good lunch
in Earlsfort terrace felt a slack fold of his belly
get no pleasure passing over her skin

spring summer smells tastes queer idea of Dublin
feeling the curbstone again the rain kept off
Dawson street lovely seaside girls floating voice
silk petticoats new garters round the body

burgundy chap in the blues Duke lane
walked towards Davy Byrne a safe man
decent quiet man downcast eyes oaken slab
curves beauty shapely goddesses

the world admires curves wild ferns evening dress
halfnaked ladies mild fire of wine kindled veins
like the way it curves there nice quiet bar
pungent mustard Bloom's heart warm

shock of air slender strips sandwich gorgonzola
tough exercise chief consumes honour parts
cheque cashed moral pub Davy Byrne's light snack
hungry man angry man spilt beer reek beery piss

stale ferment gurgling gullet saucestained swilling
wolfing gobfuls pungent meatjuice animals feed
must eat Duke street rain mucks feet holding water
in your hand walking by the Tolka travelling to Ennis

at Limerick junction squeeze a line of poetry
out of him sweating Irish stew dreamy cloudy

symbolistic esthetes loose stocking cast shadows
over coming events worst hour of the day

gloomy hate dull lines of houses miles of pavements
streets bricks stones one born every second other dying
useless words Home Rule sun rising northwest
our lovely land barmaids shopgirls hotblooded

on the cobblestones kept her voice up
must be thrilling their little frolic
a flock of pigeons encourage people
to put money by shillings pounds compound

interest twilightsleep idea forgot to tap tea
Fleet street crossing national library Dublin Castle
born courtesan drinking sloppy tea with a book of poetry
spring those questions naughty darling smart lady

oyster eyes staring dangling stick along the curbstone
from the river touched her funnybone masterstroke
the eye that woman gave her tasty dresser
shabby genteel walking up the stairs trust dream

hand rummage new moon heartscalded
died quite suddenly old friend of mine
taking out her hairpins in the bedroom
noise of the trams stream of life along the curbstone

Alderman O'Reilly emptying the port
before the flag fell out of that ruck smart girls
writing catch the eye procession marched slowly
along the gutter ordinary words sound witty

POST NO BILLS all kinds of places always
flowing in a stream a rowboat rock at anchor
swans from Anna Liffey swim down glazed apple
gaze Australians this time of year shiny

poets write similar sounds wheeling between quant
quay walls rough weather dead drunk vats
wonderful porter brewery barge sea air
O'Connell bridge potatoes poor child

house and home in their theology increase and multiply
confession absolution birth Dedalus' daughter selling off
some old furniture bluey greeny phosphorescence silver
see him hanging on the wall slow feet walked him riverward

a throwaway washed in the blood of the lamb

Aeolus

onehanded adulterer tickled the old ones
DIMINISHED DIGITS BLAME THEM
halted on pavement island peered aloft

at Nelson weary sidelong glance HORATIO
JUNE DAY plums bound for OLD MAN MOSES
Rathmines Blackrock Dalkey Sandymount Donnybrook

HELLO THERE O'Connell Street cross beauty
Penelope wrote a book against others HAUGTY
HELEN sudden young laugh wiping plumjuice

spitting plumstones DAMES DONATE striped
petticoats peering RAMBUNCTIOUS FEMALES
pull up their skirts Adam and Eve's

argue about old Dublin women on top
of Nelson's pillar RAISING THE WIND
over his shoulder young Dedalus moving

spirit walking in muck in Irishtown
caught in a whirl of wild newsboys
RETURN OF BLOOM the gentleman

at the turnstile with the blade of a knife
DEAR DIRTY DUBLIN I have much
to learn I hope you will live to see it published

a French compliment OMINOUS hosts
at Tara enjoying silence FOR HIM!
accept our culture and our language

I have been transported into a country
far away from this country
IMPROPMTU speaking the opal

hush poets frozen music the aftercourse
of our lives wellchosen words DAYS
OF YORE flinging his cigarette aside

speak for yourself RHYMES
AND REASONS for her kiss
nervous walking home through the park

nightmare from which you will never awake
CLEVER professor A DISTANT VOICE
loose neck flesh vibrating telephone

whirred inspiration before you were born
paralyse Europe lazy idle little schemer
editor nervous hand write something

YOU CAN DO IT! open gate in the park
Dublin's vocal muse Madam Bloom
gentle art Paris spleen LIMERICK

KYRIE ELEISON! westend club sofa
always loyal to lost causes a horseshoe
paperweight prince of Breffni

a woman brought sin IN WELLKNOWN
RESTURANT bullockbefriending bard
opera resembles a railway line

in copious grey of Donegal tweed
brought to every new shore
the wilderness and the mountaintop

the fat in the fire the bloody Roman empire
STREET CORTEGE hurrying out round
to Bachelor's walk EXIT BLOOM fought

the boys of Wexford hurt his knee in a hurry
COLLISION bell whirred auction rooms
page six barefoot in the hall took a reel

of dental floss from his waistcoat pocket
short and long EOLIAN HARP jigs
the editor's blue eyes opened violently

harsh voice hoarse bark of laughter
burst over the moon mild mysterious
Irish twilight does some literary work

with Gabriel Conroy a mighthavebeen
SAD and yourself? the doorknob hit
most pertinent question ate the water

biscuit looked on the sea Marathon
laughing drink some purling rill GREEN
GEM OF THE SILVER SEA entered softly

ERIN I could go home still
I am going to tram it all the way
get some wind off my chest

keys house more Irish than the Irish
bathers on golden strand
Ireland my real country

working away regret along the dark
stairs and passage the door creaked
again draymen rolled barrels dullthudding

Hades

grand morning towards the gates on the bowling green
with a lantern after death saltwhite crumbling mush
pick the bones clean some fellow that died stone crypt
how many once walked around Dublin burying the dead
expresses nothing eulogy in a country churchyard

saddened angels crosses stone hopes praying upcast
eyes Parnell will never come again mourners moved
away to read a name on a tomb blade blueglancing
mound of damp clods rose gravediggers knocked blades
on turf clay in the hole where is Macintosh now?

a postmortem caretaker moved away dying to embrace
her in the lot I bought poor mamma darkened deathchamber
lay me in my native earth the Irishman's house is his coffin
Friday buries Thursday Hamlet gravediggers profound
knowledge pretty little seaside gurls cheerful enough

corpse manure dreadful decomposing Molly wanting
to do it at the window desire you might pick up
a young widow here pitchdark night women so touchy
kiss shadows churchyards yawn sacred figure blinking
drunks foggy evening silk hats bent in concert

shook all their hands in silence a finelooking woman
a good armful his wife the soprano Lazarus come forth
last day knocking the graves damn resurrection pumping
blood a lane of sepulchres mild grey air women dead
in childbirth consumptive girls holy water the coffin

on its bier chapel door halted heaven bald holy alone
under the ground a sad case mortal agony talking of suicide

whispered glanced funerals all over the world every minute
pallbearers requiem mass death pomp curbstone stopped
cramped carriage the sexton's escape a walking tour
by the canal Athlone Mullingar Moyvalley towpath

by the lock bury them in dark red drowning grief
no more pain wake no more sunlight through Venetian blinds
awful drunkard of a wife pawning furniture every Saturday
clutching rushes in the riverbed the greatest disgrace
in the family face mauve and wrinkled death

side of the street tiny coffin the best death a sudden death
drink like the devil heart breakdown decent little man
poor Paddy! down the quay next the river over the wall
into the Liffey with sudden eagerness long laugh
pristine beauty curved hand open madame smiling

beautiful voice weeping tone pleasant her songs coming
in the afternoon under the railway bridge past the theatre
in silence mourning weather spat raindrop the grand canal
gasworks could have helped him strange feeling son and heir
in with a lowdown crowd his name stinks all over Dublin

waited waited all waited

The Lotus Eaters

womb warmth lemonyellow pale body buoyed floating languid limp
feel fresh water pleasure business nice girl perfume buttermilk
oatmeal rainwater smelling herself sweet almond oil cure
walked southward along Westland row quarter past mourning
time enough yet women enjoy it defund us archangel
and don't they rake in the money? Salvation witness confession
punish penance he saw the priest kiss the altar splendid

old sacred music gloria connoisseurs talk vibrato music
queer atmosphere priest rinsing out the chalice tossed dregs
aristocratic wine not straight men after the rosary do not deny
my request statues bleeding the Knock apparition safe in the arms
confession box oblivion crimson halters big idea nursing
newspaper and hat Latin corpse eating dying midnight
woman seventh heaven knelt heads bowed who is my neighbour?

cross and crown of thorns Saint Patrick clever idea
true religion celestials convert backdoor open hat doffed
porter churned flood flowing winding through the land
under the railway arch tore envelope tell her big dark soft eyes
she listens like cool water strange customs places
you have been forget quiet dusk feeling evening mysterious
wife perfume to keep it up Dublin voices bawled roses

without thorns love scrimmage naughty flowers language
murmuring gravely goodbye darling return to longing beautiful
name write me a long letter remember patience exhausted
punish sorry wise tabby blinking sphinx hopscotch court tenements
ruins marbles squatted child cabman's shelter curious life weathers
places no will flying syllables hummed la lala went round the corner
his son's voice! grief and misery smallpox ballad no guts

strolling towards Brunswick street quick touch
soft mark double action old man a drowning
at Sandycove get moving looking fit that's good news
kind of a tour dark lady fair man queen in her bedroom
eating bread laid along her thigh swagger abode of bliss
o yes thanks her rich gloved hand laceflare flicker display
garter settling silk stockings heavy tramcar honking

passed high brown boots fawn skin outsider gazed across the road
stylish women careless hands in coat pockets the funeral is today
get rid of him quickly as if that would mend matters overseas Maud
Gonne's letter O'Connell street Irish capital night disgrace redcoats go
sauntered across the road from the curbstone careless air cracking curriculum
thick with salt dead sea walk on roseleaves flowers of idleness too hot to quarrel
hothouse waterlilies big lazy leaves to float on with slow grace singing quayside

Calypso

the overtone following through the air heighho! a creak and dark
whirr funeral time wiped himself with half the prize story

came forth from the gloom evening hours girls in gauze
black with daggers and eyemasks poetical pink golden black shadow

strange music mirror Boylan money evening coming on patent leather
boot possessed received payment quietly Tara street picking up letters

lean spearmint file soft bounds a soft qualm regret increasing girl's sweet lips
flowing qualm spread lips kissed woman's seaside girls pale blue scarf loose

in the wind her hair troubled affection wild slim legs running remember
the summer morning shore away the burnt flesh naked nymphs

her hair down slimmer splendid masterpiece sluggish cream spirals
on the floor naked mocking young eyes Dolphin's Barn transmigration

of souls polished thumbnail search the text with hairpin stocking petticoat
in the bed what time is the funeral? flowerwater full lips letter from Boylan

torn envelope strip she set the brasses jiggling sex breaking out pert little piece
courteous seaside girls watched the butter slide and melt tuck it under her pillow

through warm yellow twilight gathered warm sunlight came running hurrying
homeward wandered far away multiplying dying everywhere born desolation

raining down foggy waters cloud cover the sun cool waxen fruit perfume
oranges olives speck of eager fire to catch up and walk behind her pleasant

to see first in the morning whacking a carpet on the clothesline her crooked skirt
swings vigorous hips nextdoor girl fresh air helps memory cross Dublin

without passing a pub good day to you lovely weather leaning in shirtsleeves
knows his business along the North Circular through the open doorway

whiffs of ginger teadust biscuitmush gush of porter homerule sun rising
in the northwest Molly's new violet garters behind the Bank of Ireland

in their dark language walk along the strand somewhere in the east Boland's breadvan
early morning delivering daily loaves a warm day latchkey hip pocket doorstep

took his hat from the peg bedstead jiggled loose brass quoits warm heavy sigh
softer sleepy grunt quietly creaky she might like something tasty in the morning

milkwhite teeth shameclosing eyes dark eyeslits her cruel nature her sleek hide lithe
how she stalks green flashing eyes coals reddening ate with relish gentle summer morning

Proteus

homing upstream turned his face on a ledge of a rock
groped in pockets handkerchief bad teeth hilt of his ashplant
seadeath seachange saltblue flash through high water

Dublin bar found drowned five fathoms toil of waters
a naked woman moon loom waves leaves sighs awaiting
flooded swaying whispering water upswelling writhing

foampool floating slops rocks wavespeech float away
rising flowing Wilde's love creases leather brooded gaze
tawny waters burning scene sun lashes sharp rocks

apple dumplings Hodges Figgis' window who ever anywhere
will read these words? white field violet night uncouth stars
livid sea rocks shadow library counter turning sun

blast banknotes paper womb pale vampire storm eyes
sea mouth's kiss bridebed moon handmaid winedark sea
tides moondrawn westering flaming sword Hamlet hat

roguewords archway trailed hair shellgrit bare feet turnedup
trousers sand slapped red carpet spread open hallway curve
slunk back unscathed cocklepickers plashing lacefringe tide

lowskimming gull hare bounding bitter waters drowning man
could not save tide flowing quickly sheeting sands cold soft
water Maiden's rock strong swimmer paradise of pretenders

enemy dog frozen Liffey famine plague Danevikings bloodbeaked
prows crested tide shoreward bones sand stones language tide
ashplant resting shut door silent tower Elsinore's tempting flood

path above rock blue dusk nightfall creeping shafts of light
cold domed room wet sand edge of the sea Strongbow's castle
Kilkenny flyblown faces outcastman peachy cheeks shattered glass

upward fog Malahide orangeblossoms facebones tobacco shreds
acrid smoke flame blue fuse burns deadly green eyes lascivious
brother Maud Gonne yoke me Ireland green fairy's fang wined

breaths slabbed tables slainte! coffee steam printer's ink gunpowder
cigarettes conquistadores gold teeth pastry wormwood slender lemon
houses sunlight bread farls mammoth skulls sand furrows south wall

come home mother father dying you going to do wonders
fiery walking proudly elbowed cabmen wild goose son
lapped warm milk crucified shirts chalkscrawled backdoors

porter-bottle stood breathing upward sandflats shipworm sieved
pebbles razorshells grainy sand green leaves epiphanies
on the top of the Howth tram crying alone to the rain naked

women! awfully holy saint never foaming mane madness
wood in the stagnant bay not beauty houses of decay
Clongowes gentry bigdrumming fists bogoak frame easy money

whitemaned seahorses stalled euthanasia taut vellum throne out
for the day from the liberties walking into eternity along Sandymount strand
wild sea money ash sword hangs boots crush shells bluesilver snotgreen seawrack

Nestor

coins dancing through checkerwork leaves
cried laughter never let in do you know why?
persecuted Ireland the bullockbefriending bard
will help fight lions on the pillars break a lance

slightly Irish homestead great humble teacher
what will you learn? you will not remain here long
you were born wrong fight for the right till the end
prince of Breffni here to our shore brought strangers

history moves that nightmare knew years of wandering
knew dishonours knew rancours wanderers on the earth
weave dying not dead gather wherever to work up
influence our history to be printed and read jousts uproar

and slush frozen deathspew spear spikes baited battling
bodies medley mudsplashed brakes noiselessly sit down
copy your literary friends the rocky road to Dublin
we are all Irish kings' sons descended from rebel blood

immortal and glorious fenians generations remember
the famine a generous people with rich delight
owe nothing pounds guineas shillings paid way
sun never sets a poet lived as long as I have wisdom

symbols of beauty and power earned treasure
of a bog stale smoky study air calling graceless
form tyrants dethroned silent stony secrets
in dark palaces childhood bends Shakespeare's

ghost is Hamlet's grandfather poor soul
heaven fox skeleton ashes mother's prostrate

body weak watery blood drained touched
the edges of a book soft stain of ink

fox burying his grandmother throat itching
answered repeated woven on the church's
looms turned the page the form of forms
tranquil brightness underworld sloth mind's

darkness the library of Saint Genevieve
your sorrow not dead weaver of the mind
amid wild drink and chapbook talk
watched with envy sweetened mirthless

with meaning laugh loudly at the name
and date shattered glass Blake's wings
fabled daughters of memory hear
space and time ruin one final flame

Telemachus

curve turning waved hand

seal's sleek brown head

on the water usurper cannot go home

throw twopence here for a pint

history is to blame an Irishman

calmly think free yourself behold

grim displeasure free thought

green stone twinkled a believer

creation from nothing farewell

ashplant quivering Panama hat

began to chant broadly smiling

tower cliffs remind me of Elsinore

sacred pint unbind the tongue

Wilde and paradoxes on the sea

bleak in wintertime this tower

money problem the symbol

of Irish art national library

thick rich milk passed long

the table a grand language

Irish to speak the sound

listened in silence old

and secret messenger

the fishgods of Dundrum

damn Paris fads the key

in the lock have a glorious

drunk astonish the druids

marrying over the sea

memories beset brooding

brain secrets amber beads

in locked drawer cloud cover

the sun moody brooding

the offence shielding gaping

wounds the memory of your mother

pray for your mother on her deathbed

say forget remember anything

what is death a dream after death

think of your mother begging you

gloomily the snotgreen sea

the scrotumtightening sea

gazed out over Dublin bay

new colour for Irish poets

bloody English bursting

with money and Oxford

dreadful ponderous mirror

propped absurd name skipped

gathering off in rapt attention

low music please pale oak face

gurgling shaking rapid crosses

in the air awaking mountains

surrounding country mounted

the dark winding stairs

intoned ungirdled

from the stairhead

Note on the Source and Methods

All of the text in this collection is taken from James Joyce's *Ulysses*. Words and phrases from the novel have been rearranged, remixed and recombined to create seventeen poems, each named for the seventeen episodes in Joyce's novel. I have not used any words that do not appear in *Ulysses*, and I have retained Joyce's spelling, capitalization and use of apostrophes, question marks and exclamation marks. The words and phrases used in the poems were randomly selected while turning the pages of the novel in reverse order, one page at a time, beginning with the novel's final page. *Dublin Wandering* is a surrealist work inspired by modernist techniques and philosophies, created as a homage to Joyce's masterpiece.

About the Author

Irish–Australian poet Nathanael O'Reilly teaches creative writing at the University of Texas at Arlington. His eleven previous collections include *Landmarks* (Lamar University Literary Press, 2024), *Selected Poems of Ned Kelly* (Downingfield Press, 2024), *Boulevard* (Downingfield Press, 2024), *Dear Nostalgia* (above/ground press, 2023) and *(Un)belonging* (Recent Work Press, 2020). His work appears in journals and anthologies published in fifteen countries, including *Cordite, fourW, The Honest Ulsterman, Howl: New Irish Writing, Mascara, Meanjin, Rabbit, Southword, Trasna* and *Westerly*. He is poetry editor for *Antipodes: A Global Journal of Australian/New Zealand Literature*.